SHRED IT!

MOBBING THE MOUNTAIN

EXTREME SNOW SKIING

Virginia Loh-Hagan

45TH PARALLEL PRESS

Ann Arbor, Michigan

www.cherrylakepublishing.com

Content Adviser: Liv Williams, Editor, iLivExtreme

Reading Adviser: Beth Walker Gambro, MS, Ed., Reading Consultant, Yorkville, IL

Photo Credits: © Artur Didyk/Shutterstock, cover, title page; © monkeybusinessimages/iStock.com, 5; © foodstck/Shutterstock, 6; © AnnaTamila/Shutterstock, 7; NPS Photo, 8; © martin SC photo/Shutterstock, 9; © Everett Collection, Inc/Alamy, 11; © k8schulte/Shutterstock, 12; © AerialVision_it/Shutterstock, 15; © Artur Didyk/Shutterstock, 16–17; © Yasemin Yurtman Candemir/Shutterstock, 18; © Cavan Images/Alamy, 19; © Action Plus Sports Images/Alamy, 20; © ericmichaud/iStock.com, 21; 22; © Taras Hipp/Shutterstock, 25; © VE.Studio/Shutterstock, 26; © GEORGID/Shutterstock, 27; © Jan Nedbal/Shutterstock, 28; © PA Images/Alamy, 29

Library of Congress Cataloging-in-Publication Data has been filed and is available at catalog.loc.gov

Cherry Lake Press would like to acknowledge the work of the Partnership for 21st Century Learning, a Network of Battelle for Kids. Please visit Battelle for Kids online for more information.

Printed in the United States of America

Note from publisher: Websites change regularly, and their future contents are outside of our control. Supervise children when conducting any recommended online searches for extended learning opportunities.

ABOUT THE AUTHOR

Virginia Loh-Hagan is an author, university professor, former classroom teacher, and curriculum designer. In college, she jumped off a bunk bed and broke her toe. No more jumping for her. She lives in San Diego with her very tall husband and very naughty dogs.

Table of Contents

CHAPTER 1

Nothing Is Impossible

Extreme snow skiers zoom down mountains. They jump off cliffs. They do backflips and turns. They jump over other skiers. They weave through trees. They zip through dark tunnels. They slide on railings. They know how to **shred**. Shred means skiing hard and fast.

Extreme skiing requires strength and endurance.

Extreme snow skiing is a type of freeskiing. Skiers **descend** steep slopes. Descend means go down. Extreme skiers make the impossible possible. They ski away from **groomed** ski trails. Groomed means prepared. They prefer **backcountry** places. Backcountry means undeveloped.

SHRED IT!

Advice from the Field: How to Fall

A ski instructor once said, "If you aren't falling down a lot, you aren't trying hard enough." Extreme skiers have to be willing to fall and fail before winning big. When expert skiers fall, they tuck their thumbs into fists. They let go of their ski poles. Spraining thumbs is a common injury. This is called skier's thumb. New skiers will try to break falls with their hands. Expert skiers know how to fall correctly. They let their whole body fall. They fall uphill. This means falling toward the mountain slope. They can stop faster. They don't have to twist as much. They also don't slide as much.

That's what extreme snow skiing is all about. Skiers push limits. They believe anything covered in snow can be skied. They jump **obstacles**. Obstacles are objects that are in the way. Skiers use obstacles to get air. Obstacles are fun but can be dangerous. But this does not stop extreme skiers!

Bill Briggs is known as the father of extreme skiing. He was first to ski the Grand Teton in Wyoming. He did it in 1971. Some areas were too steep to ski. So he used ropes to descend. Nobody believed he did it. A local reporter flew over the mountain and saw Briggs's tracks.

Extreme skiers are always looking for ways to challenge themselves.

CHAPTER 2

First Descents

Extreme skiers want to be the first to descend. They look for mountainous **terrain**, or land. They want to be the first to ski down it.

The windshield wiper turn helps skiers ski steep slopes. During this move, skiers make short jump turns. They control their speed.

Extreme skiers have even skied down Mount Everest. It is 29,032 feet (8,849 meters) high. This is the highest peak on Earth. Yuichiro Miura was the first to do this. He descended nearly 4,200 feet (1,280 m). He used a parachute to slow his descent. A **parachute** is a piece of strong, light fabric attached to thin ropes. It looks like a balloon top.

Miura is known as the godfather of extreme skiing. He even escaped an **avalanche**. This is a rapid flow of a large snow mass down a slope.

First descents started extreme skiing. They also keep extreme skiers going!

The year 1971 was important for extreme skiing. Sylvain Saudan had a first descent. He skied down Oregon's Mount Hood. It's 11,239 feet (3,426 m) high. He's had other first descents. He's the first to ski peaks about 26,000 feet (7,925 m) tall. He is called "skier of the impossible."

EXTREME SNOW SKIING:

Know the Lingo

Big air: high, long jump

Daffy: legs spread apart like a running stride

Digger: falling or crashing

Gnarly: beyond rad, beyond extreme, perfection; dangerous

Hucking: dropping off a cliff

Kicker: jumps for doing tricks

Kosak: split in the air

Mandatory air: hucking a cliff that cannot be avoided

No-fall zone: terrain that is so dangerous that a fall would mean certain death

Powder: snow

Rad: cool, radical

Run: from top of the slope to bottom, includes obstacles and tricks

Skinning: special climbing skins that backcountry adventurers attach to the base of skis that allow them to grip while going up and glide while sliding

Sick: really awesome

CHAPTER 3

There's a Style for Every Skier!

Extreme skiers love the risk, speed, and thrill. They do amazing things with skis. There are few rules. There's lots of danger.

FREESTYLE SKIING

Freestyle skiers do tricks. They do **aerials**. Aerials are tricks done in the air. They do long jumps. They do high-**altitude** drops. Altitude means height. Skiers do spins, flips, and grabs. They do as many tricks as they can. They go as fast as they can.

SHRED IT! SPOTLIGHT: Judith Kasiama

Judith Kasiama was excited by the idea of backcountry skiing as soon as she put on a pair of skis. But the more Kasiama tried to get into the sport, the more roadblocks she found. Kasiama is a refugee from the Democratic Republic of the Congo in Africa. She lives in Canada. Skiing is already a White-dominated sport, but Kasiama found that backcountry skiing was even more so. She wanted to learn but struggled to find a mentor. Then she attended a ski clinic led by experienced backcountry skier Christina Lustenberger. She learned about the sport and had fun. Kasiama started her own community organization called Colour The Trails (CTT). She aims to provide mentorship to other Black, Indigenous, and people of color (BIPOC) interested in outdoor sports. She wants to create media showcasing CTT to increase representation. Skiing and outdoor sports are for everyone!

CHAPTER 4

Keep Shredding!

Extreme snow skiing is full of risk. Chamonix, France, is sometimes called the Extreme Sports Capital of the World. Thousands of people have died in avalanches there. But extreme skiers still ski there.

Skiers must respect the mountain.

Avalanches are very dangerous. All skiers should carry **beacons**. These are devices that give off signals. Rescuers get the signals. Avalanche dogs can also help rescue skiers. They can smell people under the snow.

Avalanches are not the only danger. Mountain weather is unpredictable. Sudden dips in terrain could trip skiers. Obstacles under snow could hurt them. Skiers need to be careful of unknown terrain. Mistakes can lead to injury or death.

Accidents can happen to anyone. Extreme skiers take that risk.

Kai Jones is a talented young extreme skier. He has been skiing professionally since age 12. In 2023, he was skiing a Wyoming backcountry route when he dropped into a crash landing. He broke both of his legs. He healed and worked hard to get back to where he was before the crash. Now he's overjoyed to be back out on the slopes. Danger is a big part of the sport.

Extreme snow skiers don't let anything get in their way.

SHRED IT!

When Extreme Is Too Extreme!

Markus Eder is an Italian freeskier. He started skiing when he was a kid. But he really found his passion when he got into extreme snow skiing. Eder's short film *The Ultimate Run* showcases one long freeski run. In it, Eder jumps over chasms on his skis and steers through ice-filled caves. He glides over rooftops. He even lands in the bed of a truck and gets a short ride before launching off again. And he puts it all to music. Eder said, "I've always dreamt of finally showcasing all my skiing in one big flowy project. I love riding every discipline, so the ultimate run allowed me to bring it all together." *The Ultimate Run* is a thrilling showcase of extreme snow skiing at its finest.

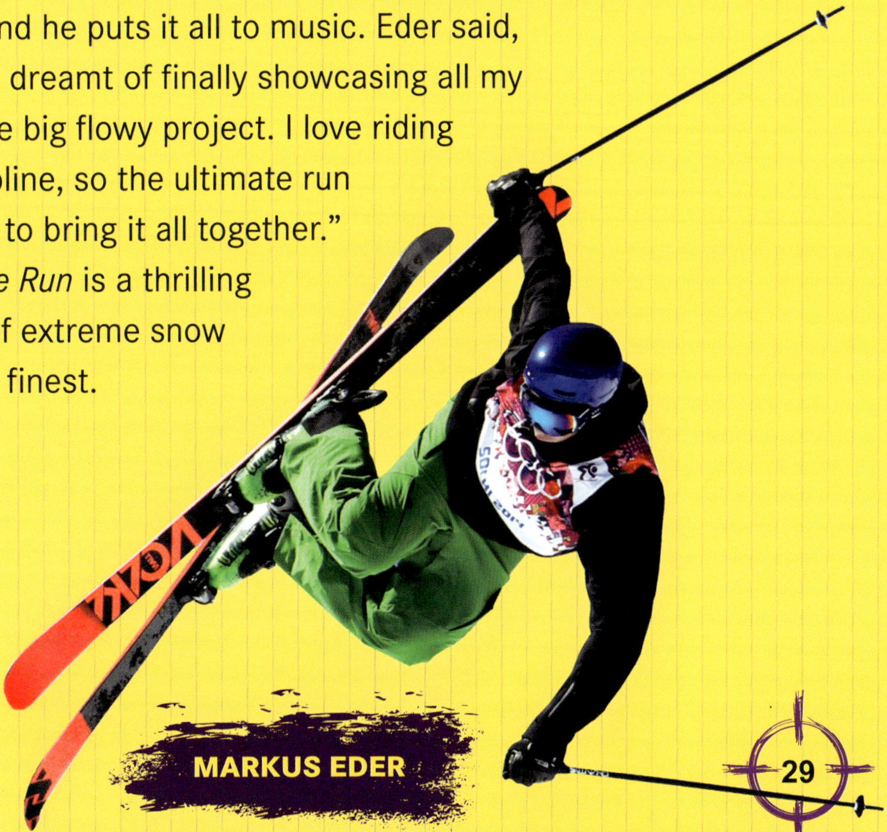

MARKUS EDER

DID YOU KNOW?

- Canadian extreme skier Sarah Burke won many medals. She was the first woman to land a 1080. It's 2 backflips with 3 full turns. She died in a training accident in 2012. She was skiing on the **halfpipe**. A halfpipe is a U-shaped ramp. She fell on her head. She then had a heart attack. In 2014 she was named a member of Canada's Sports Hall of Fame.

- Norway had a civil war in 1206. A story says that 2 Vikings put on skis. They rescued a baby prince from invaders. They skied 35 miles (56 kilometers) to rescue him. They might have been the world's first extreme skiers.

- In the 1970s, French skiers came up with the term extreme skiing. The original motto of extreme skiing was, "If you fall, you die."

- Polish backcountry skier Andrzej Bargiel set a record. He descended K2, the world's second highest peak. He skied from 28,251.3 feet (8,611 m) from the peak on the border of Pakistan and China. He did this without supplemental oxygen.

CONSIDER THIS!

TAKE A POSITION! Some skiers prefer skiing at resorts. They don't see the need to ski in the backcountry or off-piste. They think it's too dangerous. They don't think it's worth the risks. What do you think? Argue your point with reasons and evidence.

SAY WHAT? Reread Chapter 3. Extreme sports combine to form new sports. Learn about extreme BASE jumping and kitesurfing. Explain how extreme skiing is similar to and different from these sports.

THINK ABOUT IT! The National Brotherhood of Snowsports promotes Black winter sports athletes. Few Black athletes participate in winter sports. The organization lists 3 factors: geography, history, and money. What do you think about this? How could more people of color be encouraged to participate in skiing and snowboarding?

SEE A DIFFERENT SIDE! Sarah Burke donated her organs when she died. Organ donations save lives. Some people disagree with organ donation. Learn more about the different perspectives. What do you think about organ donation?

LEARN MORE

BOOKS

Hoena, B. A. *Could You Be a Big Mountain Skier?* North Mankato, MN: Capstone Press, Capstone, 2020.

Smith, Elliott. *Freeskiing and Other Extreme Snow Sports.* North Mankato, MN: Capstone Press, 2020.

WEBSITES

With an adult, explore more online with these suggested searches.

The Most Insane Ski Run Ever Imagined – Markus Eder's The Ultimate Run | Red Bull Snow | Video

United States of America Snowboard and Freeski Association

GLOSSARY

aerials (AIR-ee-uhlz) tricks done in the air

altitude (AL-tuh-tood) the height of something above sea level

avalanche (AV-uh-lanch) large mass of snow moving quickly down a slope

backcountry (BAK-kuhn-tree) natural or undeveloped places

BASE jumping (BAYS JUM-ping) an extreme sport where jumpers jump from tall, fixed objects.

beacons (BEE-kuhnz) devices that signal location

canopy (KAN-uh-pee) a special parachute for BASE jumping that looks like a bird's wing

descend (dih-SEND) to go down

groomed (GROOMD) ski trails that are prepared and established

halfpipe (HAF-piep) a U-shaped ramp

obstacles (AHB-stuh-kuhlz) objects in the way of something

parachute (PAIR-uh-shoot) a piece of strong, light fabric attached to thin ropes that slows falls

shred (SHRED) skiing hard and fast

spreads (SPREDZ) tricks that look like doing the splits in the air

terrain (tuh-RAYN) land

INDEX